Rosa Parks

Takes the Bus

By Karen Clopton-Dunson

This book belongs to

_____

Thanks to my critique partners, Matthew and Maya Dunson, Sandra Hall , Constance Clark and Vanessa Baldwin
for taking this ride with me.
-K.C.D.

SBN-13:9781974480081
ISBN-10: 1974480089

Purchase other fun history books at: www.createspace.com/3487864, www.createspace.com/3728002 ,or Amazon.com

At daybreak Rosa Parks woke up
And slowly got out of bed.

She soaked in her bubbly bath,
Then off to work she fled.

She stood patiently on the corner
And waited for the bus.
"Pay your fare and step to the back!"
She heard the driver fuss.

Rosa climbed aboard the bus
And headed towards the back.
The front seats were for whites.
Blacks sat in the back.

Off the bus she leaped.
Then into the shop she sped.
Rosa sat down for work
With a needle and some thread.

She sewed flowers on a dress,
Stitched buttons on a shirt,
Added lace to a gown
And a poodle on a skirt.

She patched up fancy pants.
Dapper suits she mended too.
Some garments were so holey,
She could slip her whole arm through.

Rosa stitched and stitched and stitched.
Seamstresses thought her work was great.
She made old clothes look brand new,
Plus her hems were always straight.

Rosa double checked the clothes,
Making sure she sewed each one.
Then put away her sewing kit.
Since all her work was done.

She happily waved good-bye
As she left the sewing shop.
And walked down the street
To the nearest bus stop.

On the bus Rosa stepped.
She spotted an empty seat,
But it wasn't in the back.
She sat down to rest her feet.

A white man wanted to sit.
So he asked Rosa to rise.
Politely she said, "No."
It took him by surprise.

Since Rosa would not move,
The bus driver came to a stop,
"If you won't give up your seat,
I will have to call a cop."

Soon Rosa got off the bus,
With a cop on her trail.

Saying no to the bus driver
Landed her right in jail.

People whispered, made phone calls
And talked to their peers.
The news about Rosa
Made some of them shed tears.

The blacks called a meeting.
Everyone had a chance to talk.
They decided on a bus protest.

They would drive, bike or walk.

They walked in the blazing heat.

They walked on a blustery day.

They walked over hills,
When the sky was cloudy and gray.

They walked and walked:
From morning till late at night.
They would not ride the bus
Until unfair laws were made right.

The busses were almost empty.
This made the drivers nervous.
If they didn't collect more money,
The busses would go out of service.

After days,weeks and months of walking
The bus laws were made new.
The blacks didn't sit in the back
Unless they wanted too.

Thank you Rosa Parks
For being brave and polite.
Because you sat down,
The bus laws were made right.

OTHER FUN HISTORY BOOKS:

The Wacky Discoveries
Of
George Washington Carver

Doctor Daniel Hale Williams in
Twas the Night of a Miracle

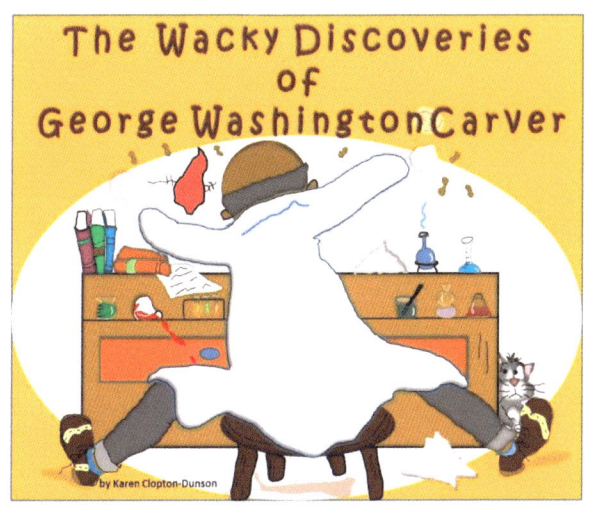

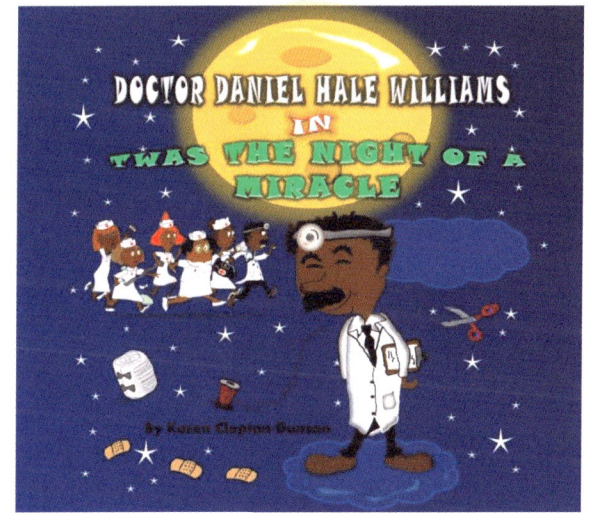